Winner of the 1999 Akron Poetry Prize

ALSO BY DENNIS HINRICHSEN

The Attraction of Heavenly Bodies
The Rain That Falls This Far

AKRON SERIES IN POETRY

Elton Glaser, Editor

Dennis Hinrichsen

Detail from
The Garden of Earthly Delights

The University of Akron Press
Akron, Ohio

Cover illustration: detail from *The Garden of Delights,* by Hieronymous Bosch, copyright reserved by Museo Nacional del Prado, Madrid

Grateful acknowledgment to the editors of the following magazines in which some of these poems, or earlier versions of them, first appeared: *Black Warrior Review:* "On a Phone Call with Two Televisions"; *The Carolina Quarterly:* "Song: Newborn"; *Chicago Review:* "Haiku (Exploded View)," originally titled "from *Scudera*"; *Controlled Burn:* "Catullus Lies in the Blue Robes of the Tiber," "Detail from the House of the Dead," "Drought Theory," "The Hundred Thousand Lines Ending in Haiku," and "Two Workshops: Timber Creek and Menlo Park"; *Crab Orchard Review:* "How Twilight Happens"; *Crazyhorse:* "Repairwork," "Replica, Shroud of Turin," and "Trash Fires Burning Up and Down the Alley"; *Indiana Review: "Hellfighters"*; *Negative Capability:* "Reel," originally titled "The Slough"; *Poetry Northwest:* "Detail from *The Garden of Earthly Delights,*" "Drawn to Water," "Perfect Pitch," and "Wave Theory"; *Third Coast:* "Orchard"; and *Witness:* "A Fish Story."

"SONG: NEWBORN" RECEIVED THE CHARLES B. WOOD AWARD FOR DISTINGUISHED WRITING from *The Carolina Quarterly.* "Detail from *The Garden of Earthly Delights*" and "Drawn to Water" received the Helen Bullis Award from *Poetry Northwest.*

I'd also like to thank the Arts Foundation of Michigan and the Michigan Council for the Arts for a grant which aided in the completion of this book.

All inquiries and permission requests should be addressed to the Publisher, The University of Akron Press, 374B Bierce Library, Akron, Ohio 44325-1703.

LIBRARY OF CONGRESS CATALOGING-IN-PUBLICATION DATA

Hinrichsen, Dennis.
    Detail from The garden of earthly delights / Dennis Hinrichsen.—1st ed.
      p. cm. — (Akron series in poetry)
    Winner of the 1999 Akron Poetry Prize.
    ISBN 1-884836-64-X (alk. paper)—ISBN 1-884836-65-8 (pbk.: alk paper)
    I. Title. II. Series.
  PS3558.I546 D4 2000
  811'.54–dc21

                                    00-056382

First Edition

Contents

in memory of Alven and Ida Van Horn

. . . solid ground gives way to marsh.
We are entering the magnetic fields
of the primal waters
of the Garden of Eden . . .
At the same time
we are entering the sphere
of radiation of the fountain of life . . .

—*Wilhelm Fraenger,* Bosch

Part *One*

ℬ *Detail from* The Garden of Earthly Delights

The smell stays longer
than the mist does,
        though the mist is prettier: backlit
and blessing the locusts
with its bride's veil,
        already the taste of pesticide
sweet on my tongue.

I note its brief passage
        across the yard, the phosphorescence
coining the grass
        with its half-lives
        and quarter-lives, its potency the yard's
payment for a stout tree.

Children scream and run
to the neighbor's yard
        awhile, their sharp cries
like blades of
leisurely daylight cutting in
        and pegging down the backyard
shortcuts, the calm

and thickening thunderhead
of shrubs.
I lean back and turn
        as the leaf buds turn,
pivot, and unfurl,
as the robins knit their crude nests

in cedar and weeping cherry,
and listen

to wind instruments turned
            percussive:
last night's rain pummeling

        and pinging
            the aluminum eaves;
    all of us—the shingles, the eaves,
                the trumpet vines
        in piggyback
up the daylit brick—expanding in the new heat.

        ℬ

        Though the locusts work hardest
                    and are the last to blossom,
            they nevertheless provide
        a pitiful display,
twin windmills gumming the zephyrs.

        The cherries, upyard, are like wild ponies,
    all bristling mane
            and a muscular crop,
        though too high up
for us to harvest.

        Only the jays feed well
    and an occasional starling.
        A wild mulberry towers
            its first green
shoots from a lower notch. I chop them out

with a dull hatchet—
the shoots grow back,
their transfer of light occurring
at the speed of light,
though whatever noise they make

is subsonic
and part of a larger rhythm: the maple
cutting its sundial wedges
into the lawn; honey bees and hornets
in loose clouds, thirty feet

high in the locusts; my daughter
down below them swinging her arms,
spotted, like a deer
in shadow,
now draped in blazing chevrons.

☙

Some days I trace with a dirty finger
the path water takes to light—
from wherever the fire is to wherever
the wires take it:
the water snapped
like a luminous rope

through the hard turns
and straightaways of the piping,
sometimes braiding
as elegantly as milk braids,

sometimes hammering
the welded joints;

either way, accumulating pressure and speed
as the pipe diameters narrow
and it leaps to steam—
twice through the fire maybe,
depending on the design—and then
a straight shot to the turbine

so that at the far end the juice can spurt
in a long, continuous spasm:
to the grids at the outskirts
of cities,
and then on to the cities,
stuffing each house with radiance
and insight:

Horace breezily flopped open
to his beloved spring;
Catullus to the infinity
of kisses that would slay him,
his "bean-pod boat" hauled out of the water
like useless ballast.

From shadow, from deepening
garden, the hose pouring
out its significant rope, my wife
finally calls to me
to shut them off
and to come
outside, there's still light in the yard.

☙

Two midmornings in June:
my grandfather finally gone
mad, the atavism spiking our zone
in the family with its haywire comet:
he's fully dressed and asleep each day

when I come to visit,
coiled like a snail
on an upturned leaf, momentarily
stunned by a shaft of sunlight
and the tipped blue lens of the sky.

Later, in the activity room, he rubs
and rubs his hands,
as if he could press away
the weakness that has struck down
each ligament and vein

in his plumber's axis—
hand to eye, eye
to mind—
until the whole grooved network
is like knotted rope, wetted down, then suddenly frozen.

☙

Late summer, the juniper bone-dry,
incendiary,
in stacked pieces

beside the barn, everywhere
      the whistle going out of the grass,

     the moist, succulent mercy . . .
       He raises his fist, and she
          takes it; he spits on his son's back,
      and his son takes it:
the old man's witness to anger

   and a withering brain. At least,
      that's what the doctors tell us,
         and they stem it more
       with drugs, long drives; but he rants on
    and begs death to sting him,

   to shake him as a small dog does
       a knotted rag, until somebody jokes
    let's return the damn gun
        and give him back the bullets,
and we very nearly do it.

     But then the mystery takes over,
    the medical guesswork:
   they zap him five times
     with a calibrated voltage,
and the clean, nuclear light

    fills his head, all the way
   from Palo, fusing it maybe,
      or reinvigorating a dormant lobe
   so the underlying rhythm
of his words is *work* again, and *walk* and *wish.*

ℬↄ

                We are simply here in the closing-
down threshold. In the contrariness
        and radial shifts
    of planet to star. I have to alternate

                between the patio and shade
   to perfect a coolness, each time eyeing,
      but from a different
perspective, the dry, though still flowering

garden. My wife, downframe,
            visibly tanner now that a strap
      has fallen,
   idly brushes some part of it

   into her cheek and brow
         so that it stains her as the sunlight
     does, seems to hold her
as she leans down

   into our daughter's pool—staggered now
      with cloud shifts,
         reflective heat—
cups some of its water along her glistening forearms.

ℬↄ

              Sappho says *a thin flame,*
       Catullus that his loins melt: nightly
   we sink to the plush
sheets, and the days burn off like alcohol.

Hellfighters

It was never the size of his penis that made them blanch, there in the
              men's room
at the Paramount,
                    but it always started there—
                                        the casual downward glancing first,
and then the slow panning upward as in the horror shows,
                                              as if to heighten
their recoil and physical revulsion.
                            You could see it how they zippered quickly,
barely glanced at themselves in the row of distorting mirrors
                                            as they raced over the
              gum-dented carpeting
to that first blast of summer daylight.
                              I know now that what they wanted was simply
              profile,
some recognizable set of the jaw to soothe them,
                                  as the movie had with Wayne's
              heroics,
all grim-faced and completely business,
                            the camaraderie of men pissing with other men
into porcelain drains,
                    but what they saw was this:
                                        the beautifully sad and girlish face
              of my mongoloid uncle,
his eyes glistening with such pure joy
                            through the haze of drugs
that it must have embarrassed them first,
                                  then stunned them to the very roots they
              held.
The complicity of it!

As if those cracked stick genes could be theirs,
the constant stress to the crown of the skull not to unwind.
It's no wonder they fought
their way to daylight,
accepted with open arms the blast furnace shock of the sun;
it's no wonder women
pushed their children
deeper onto their straws
as we ambled slowly past the incoming crowd,
always the last ones out—
he had to understand some aspect of the cranes and fires and
blasts—
besides, he craved my nickels, our bus fare home,
would drop each one gleefully
into the ticking metallic box
as if he were my guide
or father,
and this, instruction,
a casual summer outing,
as we held tight to the chrome rail
against the chop of traffic,
our palms lashed to the heat and residue
of the just-now pulled-away hands.

✍ Trash Fires Burning Up and Down the Alley

There on delicate folds of Kleenex lie our mother's
kisses, her soft
lips muted, repeated,

a hundred times it seems, and left
to sleep
there as weightless doves

until our father's Zippo snaps and they
are briefly
kited for an instant, fully liquid,

and then everywhere is fire, tongues
and sheets of
fire. I'd be punched out from flailing

at air, and sore in the ribs, so I'd just sway
in the bleeding
twilight, hauled down,

roped and knotted, swinging
by my heels
from the oak like bait or a new lamb.

In another yard, children laughing and screaming
beneath the shuttlecock.
One or two others (perhaps you

among them) painting soft jungle
landscapes
onto gray-green clapboard,

the shapes evaporating, shrinking
to ferns
and jellyfish and primitive masks,

the child molester (whose world this was)
angling
effortlessly among us, freshening

our parents' drinks, or coaxing one
of the fathers
to play accordion. Some days

I can't help thinking about that summer
coolness
everywhere, daylight hammering

in its full August fury the grain of the roofs,
the child placed
just so beside a tool,

or the body standing, muscles rigid,
so as not to graze
with bare flesh—

small of the back or buttocks, wings
of the shoulder
blades—the cold edge of

aluminum. What can it mean
to be set
fully naked at the beginning of your life

inside a garbage can, somebody's
               father pounding
          with twice-straightened nails a carport,

somebody's mother (ours?) singing
               Sarah Vaughan
          to the sunset. Somewhere

in the great expanse of evening,
               the lone
          child wandering. . . . So many thresholds:

the bird in the sky, a bluejay, the color
               of chalk;
          rain like stilettos of mercury:

you're four again or thirty.
               You lean
          toward the hose (both of you own

homes now; one of you has
               children)—
          the water shooting too hot at first

because it's been baked in the
               coil,
          but then flooding to a drinkable coolness.

♌ *Drought Theory*

I might as well be cured—as the lawn is—of all
this useless longing. I might as well be tethered down
with leather Xs—no play in the joints—

so I am nothing more than a finite number
of blades of grass, the weaving slathered over
with scooped-out mud

so it could hold water if it had to,
someone could walk two blocks south
to the river and cradle it to the lawn,

the beds of ferns—in the cup of his
hands a bleeding nest—mud staining wrists
and arms as if with birth matter.

What surrounds us is dying—birds are
dying—though she props the hose
each night until it fountains

and cardinals come, sparrows
feather in from dust-hardened branches—
evening's membrane touching us

with pale gold tailings and
a promise of stars, heaven's bony neck-
lace strung from the locusts.

I think Jesus is alive in those trees.
I think He is cradled like a caught man
or one lifted drowning, glycerined

and milked and leafed and honeyed.
What is His skin now that we might
touch Him—*the actual flesh?*

That we might place Him in our arms
or put lips to forehead
so our lips might remember

such particular salt, our arms
cull some trace of weight
or volume, skeletal density.

I shall be as careful with Him
as I am with glass. I shall lay Him here
on the lawn's parched needles

so His face is nearly my face,
redemption's face, all fakery and pigment—
I can accept this now—the play

of rouge or capillarity between skin
and fabric, my shirt soaked so thoroughly
to the armpits and wedge of back

that if the wind were blowing
I, too, might feel chilled and then evaporate.
For now, more sweat: tears and pearls

of sweat. How it stings my eyes
as I stand where the grass is dying
and pick up trash, fill pockets

and hands with it. Sun gone down now
with its green fire. A vestige of passion,
vestige of ardor—*to endure*

the flame—seeds in the understory
whispering *burn it down, burn it all down,*
for our sake. Marriage: tinder; lawn:

tinder; house, wife's body, Jesus, belief—
burn it down, burn it all down.
Inside, where it's cooler (there's

an air conditioner running; someone
has placed a faded green pail
to catch the drippings),

the new child (not ours) snuffles and
twists, then falls asleep in my arms,
his face heat-swollen, eyelids

pink-veined and fluttering.
How difficult it must be to struggle there
without language, to have no means

to cry *milk* or *hold me, there is*
wetness here, my ear is burning up,
except with fat eyes early and staggering,

indecipherable arm wags, a coarse
linen of sense strung between us. He thumbs
a cheek and cuts me, his fingernails

as quick as razors. I shall have to be
as careful with him as I am with glass.
His wants now my wants, his thirst,

as here in such witless light
(his elbow pummeling my rib cage
along that first critical boundary: *self*

and *not-self)* the dog sniffs then jets
its nostrils—breath of the invisible,
ambiguous ghost—onto the poor child's face.

✍ *Haiku (Exploded View)*

Between two sparrows
(the one in the juniper
    and the one in the glass),
    dusk sifts
its unappeasable sorrow

(or between two joys, rather,
        two suns,
it's impossible to know,
    what with one bird soldering
        pure magnesium

to the upshot breeze,
        everything turning
    mustard, pollen;
the other, smudged, reflected,
        straining late honey

from an abandoned hive).

✍

coda:

Through the temperature shifts
        and strum
    of crickets, I enter, the ferns
        against the red clay blackening,
    the nests as brittle

as fine glass coming apart in my hands;
          under the blue leaves
      of the maple,
its breath peeled back,
               the lilac nodding

  the little music it knows,
              vines breaking away
                    from the carriage barn
      of their own brittle
          volumes:

  harsh waves rubbing
        the daylight raw.
Inside, an eighty-pound bladder
          of salt's
      ripped lengthwise

          through its double wrapping,
the stones now
    in a pulverized trail
          wicking the floorboards.
There's a footprint,

          clearly a heel,
at its outside edge,
      and an interlocking braid
          of tires
leading oddly

to stairs—unrailed,
and hammered
steeply up an inside wall.
Such a provisional Eden—

the chestnuts laying pink,
now gray,
their soft, passionate
vertebrae
onto the damaged roof.

ℬ How Twilight Happens

A cloud, off-center, above the island,
the shape of the island, rides out in preparatory darkness.
The lake under it, constant, muscular.
You can almost sense the cable running through it—
ore pulled out of the earth, melted down, hardened.
It twists and twists beside us,
invades our sleep until all we know is something
of the mesh of breathing.
Your foot still cold from wading
lightly brushes the imperfect architecture of my own.
Stones flare up.
Water shifts from silver to pink—
no, grayish pink—
it floats so uneasily on the cobalt depth.
The island darkens under a peach corona.
The night's skin—*our skin*—a borderless drumhead—
begins to stain with another arc's rhythm,
building its presence from the ground up, like fog.
Roads vanish first.
Then fences, weeds.
Trees pinned to the horizon.
Tar smell mingling with pine smell mingling with lake smell.
Wind eased up now,
as if it were coming in on flatter angles.
The waves relaxed.
Water touching the edge of sand with fraying linen.
Flower scent from the side yard.
Then wind again, in gusts.
You rise to bring more of it into the room.
Pull curtains wider.

More and more of the expanding night.
More and more pine scent.
Flower scent.
How something ruby-throated may yet arrive.
To reveal, and yet, not reveal—
this sky, *that* flower; the still world.

Part *Two*

Two Workshops: Timber Creek and Menlo Park

Come, ye disconsolate, in whom any latent eligibility is left—
come get the sure virtues of creek-shore, and wood and field.

      —*Walt Whitman*, Specimen Days

All during the summer of 1876 he wrestled with the trees.

      —*Lewis Hyde*, The Gift

Whitman bent the filaments, whatever sapling
he gripped—beech or holly, hickory—
yielded its pliant fibers to his stroke-dulled flesh,

a rejuvenation and natural cure—
so why not here, St. Luke's Hospital,
Three East, the Psych Ward,

the signs of genius everywhere:
in the pool table's breakups and caroms,
in the fish tank's perfectly balanced,

air-fed stasis, my grandfather
shuffling past them from his morning's dose
to squeeze my hand in greeting.

He pumps. I wait. But no sap rises
into the ligaments and veins, no fiber and grain
into his forearm's sinew. Only radiant heat

to his body's sluggish movement, his right hand
as delicate in mine, as crushable,
as a dirt-hardened work glove.

✑ A Fish Story

Water was as good as mercury the night
I dropped the catfish in and watched it swirl,
calmly clockwise, counterclockwise,

against the pail's dented sides.
From the top it was all false volume,
wind-filled, water-filled,

as beautiful as a scarf,
some lightweight metal, miraculous alloy.
I watched it swim for hours.

Now and then I'd curve my hand
into the pail and let the dorsal,
pectoral, cut of the gill,

scrape my fingers, skinny wrist.
Even then I knew it was dying, its steel
blue the same steel blue along

my father's forearm—
witness the botched scar,
the uneasy mix of ink and tissue

where he calmly razored
until his tattoo bled.
How out of it issued (to a son)

    desire's mute howl:
Iowa farm boy, Tsing
Tao Pier, a hooker bargaining

for the gold
of his wire-rimmed glasses,
sunlight like gunshot

near the breakwater,
smell of creosote, moss, negotiation,
their reflections twisting,

bleeding silks,
on the uncertain texture
of the harbor . . .

At least, that's what I thought
the night my mother sang
and my father ignited charcoal,

the fish in the pail slowly
circling, her hands—*then fingertips*—
on the spray of his wound,

as if she could delay
what I had culled
from thin walls and ceilings,

from cracks in the door:
his quick eyes
suddenly bluing to hesitant laughter.

ℬ Reel

There came a time my father wouldn't go with me:
        too oily backwater,
    lazy Susan where they once turned

the huge engines around,
            each drunken shift
    of a boy's carnival music,

each wild horse, matted mane,
            adrift in the tidepool
    stench of creosote

and rotting timbers. To my father
        it was
    completely backlash, dialectic—

his heart's anxious flutter being shed
        of affluence—
    then pump and surge

of the daylight, the luxuriant river.
          Even then, as he baited hooks,
    he wore his white shirts,

but with the sleeves rolled
        and the collars loosened,
    the office where he computed volumes,

making boxes, just across the water.
        Across the road now
    lie houses of the poor,

their laundry dripping blue,
                    dripping Clorox. A slow,
            sure siphoning

into the bare ground. A raw transfusion. Never,
                    as the boy might say,
            a flagged brilliance

whipping in a box of sun. O city of rust
                    and tetanus,
            crushed cars, the hospital

where I was born rising red behind them,
                    its saint bruised
            and penniless

under the gunmetal sky,
                    the hesitant mercy,
            it doesn't matter now,

but a father bent once to the mess in a reel,
                    the elegant whip
            of black line

all nest and snarling.
                    The boy's hands fumbled,
            helping: such a tarnish-

able, complicitous lightning:
                    a scale
            of sunfish, smear, a counterstrike of tar.

The Hundred Thousand Lines Ending in Haiku

—for my mother's mother

What was beautiful in her arc of thought is still,
               mid-January,
         an elegance: she's cold

so she turns it up, eighty, ninety degrees,
                  before her pace slackens
        and she gazes at snow

(her hand at her throat—something fluttering;
              her mind absent-
       ly sifting columns

and wedges of daylight). There is no
            sadness in it,
       only gaps of language and her

forgetting, knitted roses pilling at her sweater's
              breastline.
       Sometimes I think the misery

is just some small nick inside the cellwork,
            some slack
       metal, noxious ore

poisoning the system, calling out to her
              as it did to him,
       with *anger,* and with such sure logic,

angelic lures, driving her naked to the glass . . .
              Once, at thirty
       thousand feet, I saw

how forgetting might work: lightning stabbing
        with such
           dull prongs the unworkable

mass, again and again, the whole sky
        lay coiled,
           stilled, all of it inverted and pointed

at heaven. Three days I've tried to
        startle her
           with memory, the purple martins

in their two-storied home, the Roosevelt dimes,
        all fled
           to some afterlife, herons stalking

the current. Here's what Narcissus wanted:
        a piece of the
           self in another made manifest,

emotion reefing the ponds and mineral
        shallows,
           something human rising

out of the networks—combustible, kinetic—
        not this
           cold narcosis, ethereal mist

because her heart, tireless engine,
        simply cups
           what it sees—a blood rose—and passes it on.

Detail from the House of the Dead

(elevator shaft: Strobel funeral home)

Only our clothes hang there now. There's
                nothing left
        of the gearwork, pulleys and cables, filigreed cage,

that first raised our town's
                dead
        from that prepurgatorial washing

to the sentencing, chapter and verse,
                in one
        of the parlors. How many

I can't say, young and old, innocent crash victims,
                wheeled over
        the terrazzo floor to be blooded dry

and harsh chemicals sluiced
                into their arterial
        runs, the mortician's callous disregard

and fussiness with cowlicks,
                the delicate weave
        of the hands,

finally killing that fear I had
                of residual
        hauntings, revenge-minded spirits.

Bats thrive here now, are, in fact,
                the only creatures
         to turn back to admire

the handiwork, which is simply us,
                sleeping.
         Early foggy March—bat in the kitchen,

bat in the den—the attic insulation
                alive
         with their clicking, to the drought-

infested weeks of early September—
                once, a single
         creature so maddened by thirst

it actually bellied down the expandable vent
                to the dryer,
         drank long from a load of whites—

shirts I wore, sheets in which we wrapped
                ourselves
         or fought, me staggering

to sleep in the other room, you waking
                and screaming
         at 4 A.M., one bat circling the bed:

omen of drift in the eye, voice;
                or star-
         shaped lump and radial webbing;

the car that floated heavily out of the Iowa dusk
the night
of my grandfather's burial.

As if we could pray to escape these ghostings
(how I hunkered
in the same room he collapsed in,

his last stroke, my head blown flimsy
and white
in the negatives); *as if*

we could screen off and tape each
chink
and vent (your voice in my ears later,

once I got home, our daughter's
voice
with its parched lips and baffling

textures)—the bats would still awaken
those
first warm, beautiful evenings,

would shoulder out of the attic
to speak,
remorseless, of twilight's

passion, its pink wash, our indelible human longing.

ℬ Perfect Pitch

This, then, was one of the city's minor boilers, and he tending it,
a cripple to the gods, though in truth he was my mother's father and kept
the upper building—Kilborn Photo—in steam and heat.

It was here, in 1958, that I first learned the undercurrent
was rhythm, stemmed in runs of piping and ruptured seals: skeletal,
celestial, a three-dimensional network feeding

our hearing. It was finally a kind of oil slung
in the inner ear, coating the hammer and anvil, the fiber optics,
greasing the long slide into the chambers

of the brain. How my grandfather could stand there listening
beyond the second set of doors and know
by the reverberations flashing across the opening

which valve needed closing, which needed opening:
his perfect pitch. And so by music, diligent labor,
he tuned machines. His territory, prewar,

during the war: parts of Wisconsin and western Illinois;
the equipment: Clayton steam generators and rotary churns,
the calculus of pressures and volumes, optimum

scaldings, registering in the gauges as pure tone,
feedback. A rhythm finally of water's making that destroyed his
hearing: the drum skin tearing and hardening

over. The hammering, hissing: dry wind
in an abandoned shaft. For a time then, laughing it off.
For a time, rising at 6 A.M. to let the birds leak in

on their particles of song, each note lashed
to a particular spot in the landscape, and he following,
his hearing aid throttled to maximum volume . . .

"O tall tree in the ear"; Whitman at Timber Creek wrestling
the saplings—my grandfather lies down now in the planet's ear, dead
stone at the center. He hears nothing

of the raucous sparrows pecking at bread crumbs. Nothing
of the bell note of the jays. Nor how the mourning
doves signal, midwire, evening, above

the tomato vines, their fluted notes the texture and purity of milk.

Part *Three*

Catullus Lies in the Blue Robes of the Tiber

Ice like tin sheeting
covers the river
so the wind is all high-hat
and a tenuous
brushwork,
an etching the snow

picks up and shuttles,
in loose scarves
and breakaway
edges, all the way to the dam.
Where the river
spills over: nothing.
Just snag ice

and twig parts, leaves
footed
in laminate. They say
the eye is stalled,
but it's not.
They say desire

curls over
like a broken body,
but it's already downriver,
staining
the current, braiding the current

in which the bullheads
hover,
turning the river's

black heart
into white meat and an iridescence.

⁊

A birthstory: moon in the skylight,
          a few high stars
punctuating the clarity.
    I come down

    out of one of the parlors
          by handhold
          and by fingertips to the plaster,
thinking of the house's

          calculable dead.
How, for thirty years, they floated here
          on silk and grief,
    the rusted gears

          of the elevator,
    their lips sewn tight,
          their arms crossed, legs
crimped, for the passage;

    what they feared, pure spirit,
          easily dispensed
through firewall, steel girders.
          Now

    nothing remains. Only
residues of absence, porcelain sinks,

their handles raised—
chrome wings—

to facilitate a cleansing.

ॐ

(Are you afaid of dying?
my daughter once asked,
then madly skipped
to an infected lawn,
hornets

everywhere the size
of my knuckles
in flowers, weeds—
a spring flashback,
salted in,
now suddenly *wintered . . .)*

Mosquitoes hover near fruit.
Early morning—
December, March—
dawn feeding the locusts

with its drugged blaze,
one troubles the fluorescence,
so I press it, bloodless,
against the paneling
as brittle as a crucifix.

Let it dry for days.

ᘒ

Catullus lies in the blue robes of the Tiber
and says nothing
of passion, but I touch him
anyway,
follow the knotted greenness

through the bones of his wrist
into the secret, feminine flesh
of his inner arm,
arm that now holds nothing
of the delicate whips

and lashings, the tongue
in frenzy
and the ointments spread, hair tasting
of salt
and of salt's vanishing.

ᘒ

Canoed downriver today:
impossible to gauge
what in the current
was new weed fanning
the bottom and

what was simply
tree rot, dying

moss, grown leathery
and plush,
a half mile above the islands.

Of where the water
shoots out, I said
nothing, my hands
pulled back
with tubercular gloves,

an evidence
I stroked unwittingly,
hand to mouth,
hand to hair,
with my careless
preening. Nor

of the bicycles
like crushed spectacles,
skeletal deer,
a child's blue tricycle
furred in petroleum,

the car batteries,
honeycombs of poison,
I knew seeped
pale featherings
to the amber current.

Everywhere now, an undulant
stillness.

Two turtles sunning,
        their shells chalk-dry
or waterlined,
        dented as hubcaps.

෮

        Minnows zipper
the shallows . . .

We fall down awkward
        to our hands
and knees, moonlight
        all over us like pieces of

cloth, pieces of map,
        a soft leoparding—
the weeping cherry
        brushing the air now

with its branch tips—
        pinwheeled, lavender—
                filaments
        and spines

        of the ferns,
    unguents and pollens: *small cries*
surface from the rear
        of the house

        (the fan still on,
            the fan blade pivoting slowly

on its one hub
and its finger's length of axis).

Minnows zipper
        the shallows . . .

And so she strides in
quietly among them,
            deeper and deeper,
her fingers avid

to touch one nibbling the flesh
of her ankles,
to lay the open secret
        of its length

        near the pulse in her wrist—
now "poor and little
            and lovely and gone"—
returned to the water.

        ℬↃ

What can the mind
accommodate of any day—
time with its
cellophane over each thing,
    bunched up

    and gumming
the narrative—screech owls

                    asleep
          in the overhang—

                    banjo music like bad religion
          drifting downstream
                    from the paddlewheel—
          God monking the grace notes?

                    ♫

          Her body like plush cloth
                    only in memory now,
          snow filling
                    the branches
          with its sham tree,

                    the trunk bamboo
          and willowy,
                    none of it linear,
                    though the crows raucous
          west of the house
                    have moved narratively

                    to the east—
          a tense change
                    but with the same
                    point of view
          (the cardinal asleep

                    in the mugo pine)—
          one jay circling now,

as dense
as an afterthought,
its shadow juking, feeding,
then jumping expertly away.

℘

Insulin beads on the grass blades,
cool tongues
sheathed in greens
and platinums.

I keep smelling
new paint
drying,
which are the lilacs:

crimped wires smoldering
in a crystal
vase: the heart
on fire, the mind in fidelity

to the many gods:
a stranger's T-shirt once
so magnificently white
I could put my hand right through it.

Part *Four*

♪ Song: Newborn

When I held her up to the light and the light held,
angling lazily over the pond
and congested rotary,
I could already see the impurities that would take her,

could already see the new flesh
smeared
by the oil of my hands,
could feel, against my cradling arm, her lungs straining like twin
pumps
against the corrosive tides of air.

I always wonder if she twinged when the city buses
passed,
filling our house with the scent of fuel,
or if she locked easily, quickly,
to the alternating rhythm of traffic and ocean breezes,

because even
the body's other engines must wear in,
accommodate themselves to the pace
of an accelerating heart, no bigger than a tea bag,
but furious in its pumpings.

The city buses worked late into those summer evenings,
marked our lives with the haze of diesel and boiling tar
that I inhaled and coughed back up
as I woke nights to console her.

And as I sang,
she calmed,
the buses ripped seams the length of the street in predictable intervals,
my nose just grazing the perfect, healing unguent of her hair.

✍ Drawn to Water

(near the wastewater treatment facility)

So this is where the used condoms swirl,
       as pale
    and blind as deepwater

fish, of desire slackened; wads
       of Kleenex,
    leaves: butterflies and moths

in sugary amber; all around the three-staged
       ponds
    oak roots angling in,

seeking the cracks and leachings. Downstream,
       di-
    aphanous webbings,

swags of ether. Idle Sunday, they hold
       me in
    and hold the river back

so it can heal me, good horse spangling
       the drop-
    through, can bless our town's poor,

who are here now fishing—
       they eat
    what they catch—with its skewed

anointing. They're up to their ankles
                in the river,
                        muttering Chinese and Spanish, a beautiful-

ly damaged English, sunlight hesitantly
                reddening
                their bare necks and open collars.

I could quote them Ovid, maybe. Describe
                the metal-
                lurgical blur in a drop of lake-

water, or what floods from the sewers
                when it rains
                hard here, and they'd just laugh and lay

their soft arcs back across the water, reel them in
                with a whipsaw
                ratcheting. And they're right,

maybe. The contaminants are inlaid elsewhere,
                risen,
                wafer and tongue, to another

cool precinct. They're not here in the day-
                light
                spilling upstream

its skid of lumber, not in the soft,
                methodical
                thrashings of the paddlewheel. It's different

now that it's afternoon. I should talk
                    instead
            of how an April heat's

spiked early, the forsythias
                    ablaze
            in a fury of pollen, the nights

gone dry mouth, gone cotton-
                    mouth,
            too sudden. How waking, we splash

ourselves with chilled, expected
                    purity,
            gulp it down by the handfuls.

ℬ Repairwork

(Shroud of Turin)

They must have bled as they sang,
the needles so quick through

the linen, the frayed mesh,
the silvers must have stung them.

Pinpricks they must have stemmed
with their tongues, unembarrassed,

these brides of Christ—
like sewing patches of sunlight

to water—the ghost in the cloth
laid double across their laps.

These are the hips of Christ,
knees raw bone inking the linen;

this, the stain of a coin
that graced His eye, the image

as yet unpatterned, available only—
should they dare to look—

in random angles, stitches.
Terrible gash at a medial rib.

Imprint: sole of His foot,
the other merely heel, curve of

a branch at its one end blackened,
released to ash—their

fingers as furious as sparks
in the medieval dusk

repairing a fire . . . They must have
wept as they bled as they sang.

ℬ Wave Theory

Blue and silver at first,

then white washing through with presence,
            no one speaking,

the twisting, turning one, the one hidden, veiled,
                quietly singing
            in her evening bath. Imperfect skin—

he held her once—age showing everywhere. Sculpted wood
                and memory of rib cage, the
            undulations not themselves but of

some deeper movement, as deep
                as thought
            or memory. Time scalloped and

lingering bell note. Their faces hidden—always—
                the looks
            on their faces. The sound of them in the dark

(because the child was near) like a bather's quiet singing.
                The story he might tell
            is this: bees

lived in the walls, made honey—all summer and then
                winter, another summer—
            until the weight of it undid the nails

and the plaster melted, broke apart in sheets, and
                the honey
            spilled in one towering, golden wave.

He does not touch her now. The one hidden, the one
                    veiled,
          now present in rational aspect.

Geese wheeling above them, the geese so high up
                    they are vaporous cutouts.
          And so he reconstructs from fragments,

lives in his fingertips—all summer, then autumn, winter,
                    another summer—
          hands on thigh; tongue and nipple;

the manic kissing spreading the other's wetness,
                    the self-made wetness,
          from hand to tongue and lip and mouth. *Wave*

theory. A theory of husbands; wives. He wants to know:
                    when a wave
          crashes its whole length—at least here—along

a curving longitude, and then rushes back,
                    otter-slicked,
          greased, so that part of it is silence and

a memory of wave, which part then is cure
                    to the already
          pulverized shoreline? Which part wound?

The wave dissected reveals nothing of its inner
                    structure.
          It is heartless, organless. One

solution cascading as variable into another.
The crashing
a chamber where they spoke and walked.

The wind itself companion so that it lingered
in her hair awhile
so that her hair moved as scarves move—*wait,*

he has this wrong, her hair was shorter then—
it was a scarf that moved,
or the wind in her blouse

so that each gust pressed it closer, wrapped it tighter,
the rain assisting,
matting it down, so that she was

self-contained inside the weather and each word
she spoke—
which was her happiness shouted back

to him—was as if muted by the fabric.
Blue at first, then
silver, then white washing through. A dictionary

of sand equations, drought theorems: *he buys*
a ring
in the New Mexico desert sculpted with waves,

feels married to water.

ℬ Orchard

What he missed most afterwards was talking in bed,
                                        her voice chilly
at first, but still between them—

as if someone had set in the middle of their sleep
                                        a plate of freshly
picked apples—

white coals of daylight,
                        the skins still taut.

How one of them would idly touch one
                                and then set it back
on its bottom crown so that it slightly rocked.

Or bring another to the lips as if to kiss—
                                but not kiss,
not nip or bite.

The smell of the trees
                all around them.

The plate still cold: brittle stoneware.

The flesh which was not flesh
                        slowly warming in their hands.

ℬ *Replica, Shroud of Turin*

Midmorning, the end of May, I stand
        before the Xerox
    of the residue

of the body of Jesus, His linked bones
        bled
    into the tripartite linen

by something patented, no doubt, robotic,
        though there is something still of cut wood
    and resin in it—

wet sticks pressed to the cloth—
        or perhaps just chalk ground down
    and mixed

with umber, the grained pigment
        siphoned through a fisted hand,
    gravity tearing apart

the downward twisting feather—
        a rubbing taken of nothingness—
    somebody calm at the outskirts,

gently blowing as if to reveal the rigidity;
        another erring slightly
    above the linen,

his hand tracing, then scumbling
        the length of a femur (the negative
    elsewhere, the black

Christ elsewhere) . . . *It's later; I'm home.*
                My daughter is playing rhythm
and blues music again

        in her room in the dark, the hip-hop rap-
                ture converted to sound
in the laser's blue spike, converted

        to what I think is her slow dervish.
                She vogues
where no one else can see her,

        or just plain shakes her hair,
                the god in that wobbling axis,
styled, innocent.

        Then silence, another clean sound,
                no dust
in the spaces, heavy bass.

        Her sweet falsetto drifts, tentative at first,
                but then pure seeking
as she narrows the range,

        the lyrics there, then not
                there (a neighbor's listening),
then phased, asynchronous—

        I shall sit down now, I shall not fight back—
                through birdcall—
such reverberations—the rustle of leaves—echoes.

ॐ On a Phone Call with Two Televisions

Now yesterday's riot streams over the current
as an ongoing
now: the man already bled

but there again bleeding
in the Los Angeles blast zone,
crawling on stunned hands

in front of his truck, the good eye hovering,
nearly weightless
in its turning back over

to record our trance: *side of the foot to the stomach,*
a concrete block
unbelievably raised

and brought to the head . . .
My father just keeps on talking,
for his part, watching

pornography—a man and woman groveling
ever louder
into his partial deafness

so his nerve ends snap and his heart thrashes
like a sunfish
in his hooded chest. What can I do,

but listen? Through the grains and spun
strands
of the cable—the planet's groundswell,

riots of yellow pollen
              shifting like great seas
        in the wind; in the nest

of my ear, the distortions
              of AT&T
        whistling, subsonic, like a sprouting

grass, all of it in fragments
              and accidents
        of attention, a crude sampling

arguing *spirit,* each man gluing one side
              of his hearing
        brain to the miraculous pixels.

Pornography and deafness, murder-
              ously good
        fucking and deafness—a pale blue spider

darts here, not there,
              beside the blood-red
        coffee mill. To its elemental phlegm

my daughter thumbs it,
              says it's time
        for school—my father just keeps on

talking—over the commercials
              and political lip sync,
        holding up each new surgery's harvest

like a string of perch, the local weather
                  indistinguishable
        from the rioting

and his dying, my working my daughter's
                  school lunch
        into the process—

I've soft bread in my hands—
                  her walking in later
        to butterfly a kiss into the matrix. *Something,*

something . . . My television clicks. A voice-over
                  prints through the shine
        of my ear: it's my father

gasping to say it's spring again:
                  in Iowa,
        just now, a goldfinch has landed in his maple.

Notes

Detail from *The Garden of Earthly Delights:* The title refers to the middle panel of the Bosch painting, *The Garden of Delights,* though not to any specific detail in that panel. The quote in section three is from Catullus, poem #4, *The Poems of Catullus,* translated by Peter Whigham. The quote in the last section is from the Sappho fragment beginning "He is more than a hero," translated by Mary Barnard. The paraphrase in the following line refers to Catullus's translation and use of this fragment in his poem #51. Kenneth Quinn speculates, in *Catullus: An Interpretation,* that this was the first of the Lesbia poems.

Perfect Pitch: The quoted phrase is from *The Sonnets to Orpheus: First Series,* poem #1, translated by A. Poulin, Jr.

Catullus Lies in the Blue Robes of the Tiber: The phrase quoted in section six is from "Piccolini" by James Wright (*To a Blossoming Pear Tree,* Farrar, Straus and Giroux, 1977).

About the Author

Dennis Hinrichsen, a native of Cedar Rapids, Iowa, lives in Michigan, where he teaches at Lansing Community College. He has a BA in English from Western Michigan University and an MFA in creative writing from the University of Iowa. He has previously published two full-length collections of poems: *The Attraction of Heavenly Bodies* and *The Rain That Falls This Far*. Among his awards are a fellowship from the National Endowment for the Arts, grants from the Michigan Council for the Arts, and prizes from *The Carolina Quarterly* and *Poetry Northwest*.

About the Book

The Garden of Earthly Delights was designed and typeset by Kachergis Book Design of Pittsboro, North Carolina. The typeface, StonePrint, was designed by Sumner Stone in 1991.

The Garden of Earthly Delights was printed on 60-pound Writers Natural and bound by McNaughton & Gunn of Saline, Michigan.